SHORT TERM RENTAL SUCCESS

STORIES FROM THE EDGE VOLUME 1

Conquering and Crushing Fear in Today's Sharing Economy

2018 EDITION

M2 Asset Publishing, Inc.
Av. Mutualismo 1321
Independencia 22055 Tijuana, B.C. Mexico

All rights reserved. No part of this book may be reproduced, stored in a retrieval system or transmitted in any form or by any means- electronic or mechanical, photocopying, recording, or any other- except for brief quotations in printed reviews, without prior permission from the publisher.

Success Stories from the Edge (series and concepts), T.E.R.M. ®2008 and their Logo and Marks are Trademarks of Matt Malouf.

Although the author, co-authors and publisher have made every effort to ensure the accuracy and completeness of information contained in this book, we assume no responsibility for errors, inaccuracies, omissions, or any inconsistency herein. The information in this book is sold without warranty, either express or implied.

ISBN: 9781981050765
2018 Edition
Publication Date: May 2018
Version 1 © Copyright 2018 - M2 Asset Publishing, Inc

Dedication

To my beautiful, loving and supportive spouse Gladys, whose support and strength inspire me each and every day. To my kids who make life meaningful and worth living, thank you Andrew, Edward, Roxxane, Cally, Elon. Also an extended thank you to the rest of my family and friends whose support and encouragement are appreciated everyday even if that list is too long to mention here, you know who you are. Love you guys (and gals).

FOREWORD

We face countless decisions daily. We all do. Many are small and trite and meaningless. But there are a few that are meaningful and can either move one forward or retard growth.

How do we make these decisions? Generally speaking, we use heuristics (as defined by WikiPedia):

A heuristic technique, often called simply a heuristic, is any approach to problem solving, learning, or discovery that employs a practical method not guaranteed to be optimal or perfect, but sufficient for the immediate goals. Where finding an optimal solution is impossible or impractical, heuristic methods can be used to speed up the process of finding a satisfactory solution. Heuristics can be mental shortcuts that ease the cognitive load of making a decision.

So, we tend to do what we've done in the past because that is our internal guideline of what has worked. However, is that the MOST OPTIMAL way to perform?

What if your natural response (like most humans) tends to lean towards "conservative" or "risk averse" and therefore, you are missing tremendous opportunities?

The first step, I believe is to surround oneself with people who are trying new things. Learning. Making mistakes. But making forward progress.

This smaller 'tribe' of folks are very optimistic.

Which, is also quite encouraging and comforting. Even in the face of adversity, mistakes, losses, and other "bad things", they remain upbeat and continue to try, iterating, until they get it right. And, eventually, they do!

But, most importantly, they are changing their outlook in life. All of a sudden, their heuristics are no longer risk averse. They are open to new ideas and opportunities. And, they hone an ability to take small risks which gradually over time, begin to shift their life and lifestyles.

Matt Malouf has put together a collection of such contributors in this book. It is well worth reading as everyone shows vulnerability and fear. And, how they personally recognized this fear (which is the first step) and then consciously expressed a desire to change.

I'm thrilled that I've created a "safe" environment on Facebook, YouTube and through our online membership for like-minded ordinary people looking to stretch their wings and experiment in a safe zone with guidance, friendship, mentoring and a growth orientation.

Read their stories (please) and see what resonates with you.

Are you interested in growing? Are you scared (it's highly likely you feel anxious about taking the next step or find reasons not to do it. "The time is not right. I don't have the capital. I don't have time. I heard of someone who lost a lot of money". Whatever the excuse is, it doesn't matter - it resonates with you personally and prohibits you from moving forward. It is real.

Come hang out on the other side of the fence. One where we view opportunities with optimism and instead of avoiding risk, we begin to embrace it, slowly, methodically, holding your hand throughout. Baby steps.

I personally have achieved the success I have by having a divergent viewpoint.

Risk is my friend.

Because everyone else eschews risk, it is mispriced. And, like being the "House" at the casino, if I take enough calculated, smart risks, at the right time, and price it correctly, over time, I win. My heuristic that I lean on with every decision is to accept risk and actively seek it out. I'm not a daredevil.

I'm not foolish. But, I am self-aware that I can grow personally and professional faster and further by embracing calculated risk. And, once I realized that, my life changed.

I encourage you to read this book. Join our free Facebook Group (https://str.university/community), subscribe to our free YouTube channel (@struniversity) to learn how to monetize the roof over your very own head and get started with minimal risk. We'd love to have you and help you grow!

I leave you with a quote from "The Greatest":

"He who is not courageous enough to take risks will accomplish nothing in life."
-**Muhammad Ali**

Best,
Richard Fertig
Founder of Short Term Rental University

The success strategy to reading this book

Here's my simple advice on how to get the most out of reading this book:

Commit to one chapter a day.

That all folks. Each chapter is approximately 1500-2500 words and should not take more than about 15-20 minutes to read. A chapter is easy to do, but it's also easy NOT to do. Which is why we want you to commit. Each author and contributor took time out of their busy lives to commit. They took time away from their business, from their families to commit to expanding the human experience by sharing their trials and tribulations here. They took a leap of faith, keyboard and poured their heart and soul out here.

Here's how I define commitment:

Doing what you said you would do because you said you would do it, through thick and thin, regardless of the odds and tribulations.

If you're willing to give up on any excuses and commit to just one simple chapter a day, you will begin to see a shift in your short term rental business, a shift in your attitude, a shift in your life. We all face challenges and adversity in life, it happens, especially in your short term rental business. Come and take a journey with us on how these everyday folks like me and you overcame some of the biggest fears and challenges to achieve a breakthrough in their short term rental business to then improve their lives.

What did I do to go from nothing to achieve a wonderful life full of love, opportunity and hope? I took small steps, each and every day towards my perceived goals, and when those goals changed? I adjusted myself and my thinking to meet the challenges ahead. Most importantly I drew support and inspiration from those around me who overcame similar issues to design a fulfilling life worth living, a life that makes a difference.

Becoming just 1% better each and every week will drastically change your outlook and lifestyle.

Short Term Rental Success Stories from the Edge is a breakthrough in the short term rental market. Rather than publishing a 50,000 word treatise on how you can make all this money on short term rentals and travel the globe on 4 hours of work a week, we went in the opposite direction. We reached out and found some of the best thought leaders around, action takers who took a leap of faith to make their dreams come true through commitment, hard work and action.

Each of our experts has made an art form of achieving their success in the short term rental market by facing and squashing their fears in the face of adversity. Each has written a powerful and moving chapter allowing you some insight into their heart and soul about overcoming fear to challenge oneself and come out on the other side better. A better host(ess), a better guest, a better entrepreneur, a better family member.

Each of our authors has agreed to lay it all on the line and hold nothing back. Every one of them has made a commitment to your success by sharing their hardship. Should you find a particular author or authors who impact you, please feel free to reach out to them through their contact information provided at the end of their chapter.

I would also like to thank each and every author who contributed their valuable stories and experiences to this project. Thank you so much Gladys Jeannette, Crystal L Reed, Jeanette Lytle, Kathy Hansen, Kevin Borgersen, Kim Ottone Tank, Thao Kuat and Tom Blouin. Who, without your hard work and leap of faith this wouldn't even be possible.

Let me be the first to say thank you from the bottom of my heart for helping me mark something off my bucket list and for picking up this book. Now is the time to get committed, to conquer and crush those fears to be the success we all know you were meant to be.

-Matt Malouf

CONTENTS

AirBNB Can Help Homeowners into a Home? 1

Can AirBNB Change the Fortunes of a Village? 7

LEAP AND THE NET WILL APPEAR 15

The Accidental Hostess 25

My Harmony Hideaway 32

No Time for Fear; Too Busy Making Guests Happy 38

MY JOURNEY TO HOSPITALITY 46

The Reluctant Host... 55

Choosing To Be The Best 63

AirBNB Can Help Homeowners into a Home?

There's actually many people that don't do any kind of investment due to the fear of not knowing if "IT WILL WORK" but as in many other industries there is never a sure way to know these things? Like REALLY? Weather it's in a Restaurant business, Boutique, Coffee Shop or even an Ice Cream Truck, who can or does actually guarantee success in a Business?? Not even an attorney who gets paid to represent the public on a simple ticket can guarantee an outcome—they will say that they will TRY but that is it!! So how does this relate to Real Estate and AirBNB you ask?? Well it is ALL a RISK, only Real Estate has the highest payback and benefits. Starting with of course the tax write offs which many of us now a days actually need or flat out want in a big way.

The trick is how can you efficiently and in the most affordable way get these properties, if you're not the kind of person that would want to rent a room from your own house? Or maybe you don't own a house and just want to purchase it for the sole purpose of running an AirBNB business. How does someone start this all together? I've heard questions like: what if the place I get is too big and I can't manage it? What if it's too small and people won't like it? What if it's in the city and people thinks it's too noisy? What if it's out in the mountains and people think it's too far? What if? What if? What? If? The simple answer is. There is a person for every rental out there just like there's a buyer for every home out there.

As a Real Estate Agent based in Southern California for over 20 years now I've heard, seen (and want to un-see) just about every scenario you can imagine involving jobs, human resources, family arguments and issues to cash rich under the table side jobs, and everything in between. Some that were so simple to fix, some that were treated as if the world was going to end and some that were so incredible that made me question the direction and reason of me staying in this industry BUT………. I stuck with it and here we are still alive and selling Real Estate. So basically nothing scares me at this point. I just heard a saying this morning which was "Many people have Bad Days, Bad weeks and Bad years but Entrepreneurs and Successful people have bad moments". This hit home for me because we all go through our own ordeals, some big some small. What matters is the way we react to them. We don't have the Luxury of Staying idle for ever. As a business oriented person we have to always keep moving forward make the best decision from the options that we have at the moment and choose to make a decision and make it work and if it doesn't work we will adjust as needed.

So now on to the Real Estate talk about this Chapter… READY??

As a 1st time home Buyer you have many benefits given to you by the Government. Some lenders will see if you qualify for a ZERO down payment loan, which DOES have an income cap since it is to help people that aren't Millionaires per say. It does have different qualifying requirements depending on the house hold and income. The lender will let you know what the income cap is depending on the amount of members in the house hold. In the past 10 years I've only had 3 people that did not qualify for this programs income cap. These people didn't really NEED it but wanted to see if they qualifies just so they don't have to pay the down payment. For the record they did have the down payment but just didn't want to shell out 10k if they didn't have to.

This 1st time homebuyer program is an FHA product and DOES require the owner to live in the property, so for this property you should definitely be thinking about renting a room or two for your business. As an agent I always ask for credits from the seller which would be a certain amount of closing cost and or a request for a Home Warrantee (more on this later). It would be up to you to see how much you would like to ask for as far as credits. Many lenders also do lender credits, so always think about that before asking for Seller credits. The cleaner any offer is with ANY kind of loan the better chances are that it will get accepted, by cleaner I mean the less requests we make from Seller. Just put yourself in the seller's position and think what type of offer you would accept. If you were the seller, does this offer make sense?

Another type of loan that my buyers get is the 203k loan which is the loan many buyers that want to buy a CHEAP fixer upper get. This loan does require a down payment, depending on which lender you get, it can be as low as 3%. The lender will be the one that narrows it all down once they do their numbers. With this Loan you can get a Bank owned home or any home that is in definite need of SOME TLC. The good thing about it is that these loans require you to get a Licensed Contractor that knows their stuff and they get paid through escrow so as the work gets done they get paid. This is a good deal if we're able to find a home in a fairly nice area but would be too expensive to buy at full retail. This loan also an FHA loan which requires for the owner to live in the property as which any FHA loans.

There's also conventional loans that definitely don't require you to live in the property so the options are there.

We are currently working with a Lender that will help you qualify for a purchase of a home, and guarantee that your AirBNB Business starts off on the right foot. They will advertise the listing for you so you can start earning money as a host right away and get your short term rental business started correctly. Yes you heard that right, we can get you qualified with AirBNB income to get you a home, exclusive to us.

The above are only a couple types of loans, remember that there is also seller financing and option loans that let the buyer rent the property 1st before having to buy it. There's so many scenarios of financing it will definitely be a case by case basis and also what your circumstance is. We're ready to help you decide what will work for you. Personally I would look for a seller financed property—no banks and no fuss. These sellers are the ones that own more than one property and would be renting one no matter what. Some want to sell but don't want to go through the hassle either! So it works for both of you. The best part is there aren't ANY restrictions for your AirBNB business.

One of the 1st things aside from insurance that I will recommend is to have a great Home Warrantee company. These Warranties cost on average about $500.00 but are worth so Much more. For example when we moved into our new home 2 years ago within about two months half of the lights went out in our new house….HALF!! The only thing we were to pay for was the service call which was $75.00 and they fixed it. Apparently the breaker box that we had was not enough for the amount of outlets we had on one particular side of the house. It turned out to be a close to $2,700 bill at the end which we didn't have to pay.. BUT before that our dryer stopped working, the shower had hot water and the stove was working fine but the dryer wasn't drying. I was Pregnant and had a Toddler so we needed this to work. Lucky we had a Home Warranty that the seller paid for. We had someone come in and the gas had stopped coming into the dryer

So what are your questions? What are your fears? I can go on forever going over scenarios. Do you need help in locating a property? How can I be of service to you? I have many resources for you! Lenders, Insurance Companies, Home Warranty Companies, Inspectors, and Contactors the list is long. If you've been thinking about investments this is the perfect time to start your AirBNB Business. Start in your own home and see how it works the logistics and as you know there are plenty of groups out there that help each other with even the smallest questions, for example "what towels to use" remember that we all start from a certain point and it can only get better from there. The support is out there to all we need to do is ask.

Remember you can be a host anywhere in the world, just start off with a plan a little organization, systems and a comfy bed. For now I can help you with properties anywhere in the United States and have lenders that are licensed throughout the states as well. I'm very investor friendly since I flipped homes before I know that scary feeling first hand. Once you go through your first deal it will all be easy, I'm here and available for any questions you might have.

About the Author

Striving to excel in the competitive world of entrepreneurship!

Entrepreneurship is a lifestyle and Gladys Jeannette is a firm believer in this fact. Entrepreneur by nature and by choice, Jeannette has built her business from scratch. Being a single mom, she had her children to think of and that kept her going even when the times were tough. She made her kids the first priority and has never regretted that decision. Now she's busy running successful real estate and digital marketing businesses that are geared to aim for the stars.

Jeannette is a thriving member of Excellence Real Estate and works as their Operations Manager. Her passion for real estate and her love for helping people allowed her to excel in this role. Her commitment to her business and profession is apparent through her work ethics. Known for her straightforward manner, Jeannette is known by her clients as the woman who gets work done! She is a firm believer in delivering results as committed; a trait that has allowed her to attract a diverse clientele.

Having over 20 years of experience in the trade, Jeannette knows the market inside out. Her attention to detail and work ethics have allowed her to get the competitive edge. Some of Jeannette's recent training include California Agency, Real Estate Law, Risk Management, Trust Funds, Code of Ethics, Asset Management, Fair Housing, Tax Favorable Real Estate, and Environmental Hazards. Working to succeed in the real estate industry isn't an easy task but Jeannette, pushed on by her strong resolve have managed to make a name for herself.

When not assisting clients, Jeannette spends her time with her kids. She also travels to Guatemala every year and helps one of the villages there. They are like her adopted family and Jeannette wishes to invest more of herself in the cause.

Gardening is another one of her hobbies and she has an edible, exotic, and tropical garden. They are her outdoor babies and even after a busy day of business and family, Jeanette makes sure to spend some time taking care of her plants.

Please visit Gladys Jeannette at: http://ierealty411.com

https://www.facebook.com/EXCELLENCE411/

Can AirBNB Change the Fortunes of a Village?

Okay you and I both know that money doesn't grow on trees. We work long and hard for it to make something for ourselves and our family, especially when we near retirement. This is why so many of us are so terrified of investing our money anywhere, let alone in an entirely new town, or village, or even a different country.

But if you set aside the risk and benefit factor, don't you think investing in real estate in a village can actually turn all odds in your favor? Where investing in a village's real estate might be scary, don't you think NOT doing so would be even scarier?

I honestly find it a petrifying to think about just sitting there and letting my money sit in a bank account earning a paltry 0.05 percent or something along that line when I could be receiving a far more lucrative return on my investment along with some nifty tax benefits. After being involved in over 100 investment opportunities over the course of 20 years, I have niched down and now specialize and endorse the idea of investing in "bolt-hole" properties. A bolt-hole property is a property of any kind (most often in a second or third world country) that you can acquire for less than USD$15,000 including all commissions, fees and taxes associated with the transfer. These properties are actually affordable and offer a perfect getaway destination or retirement abode for people from the first world countries to enjoy a peaceful residence, away from the hustle bustle of the urban life. These types of deals are NOT for everyone, they require a bit of a pioneering and wanderlust soul who is comfortable thinking outside the box and doesn't require all information handed to them on a silver platter. You'll need to get down and dirty so to speak.

I agree that you will have your concerns. You might not be able to enjoy all the facilities that you are used to in the city. This is the whole point of having a bolt-hole property a place in a village with a population less than 10,000 people. You get to enjoy a residence that is away from the buzz of the metropolitan and into the peace and tranquility of nature. A place that has all the basics covered for simple, satisfying, tranquil living. What more can you dream of when you have a shelter, water, food, proper infrastructure, and a caring community surrounding you?

Anyway, we need to look at the bigger picture. We need to enjoy the rewards of life, but also find a way to give back to the community, to make the world a better place through our investing and I honestly believe that AirBNB or short-term rentals can actually transform the fortunes of local towns and villages located on the off beaten paths, leading them towards growth and prosperity.

Let me tell you a little about my own experience. Not too long ago, my family and I decided to invest in a property, located in a tiny lakeside village at the edge of the rainforest in Central America. This village is located next to some of the largest and noteworthy ruins of the Mayan Civilization. The village has a population of about 3,000 residents.

I understand that investment is not as easy as I make it sound. If anything, it is actually a quite scary thought if you sit down and evaluate, there are just so many things that can go wrong with it. But that happens with literally every business venture, doesn't it? Risk and fear, does that mean you quit trying and just sit back at home because of this?

ABSOLUTELY NOT!

And why should you focus on all the things that can go wrong with property investments in short term rentals in villages and local towns when there are so many things that can actually go right?

Initially, we bought this property in the Central American Village as a part time retirement abode. It was located in a quiet area, engulfed by natural scenery, and a small, caring community. For our retirement, my family wanted to move to a place that was quiet but still had a sense of belonging like we were a part of a community and this place has a feel that American neighborhoods did half a century ago a la "Leave it to Beaver". We did not want to completely isolate ourselves but we also sought solace. The peace and quiet this place offered gave us a perfect balance of both.

Nevertheless, there was still plenty of time until retirement and we had already bought the property (sight unseen which I don't recommend very often by the way). So for us, it was just sitting idle. We did not want this property to remain vacant and be an eyesore when so much could be done with it. Buy what?

We thought about what could be done with the property to save it from sitting empty. So to get a better understanding of all the options we had, we decided to talk to the locals since they obviously know more about their area than we do. Usually renting to locals can cause more difficulty than you would want as an absentee landlord so we continued to explore the possibilities, reading, researching and walking around talking to locals and meeting people. We wanted a solution where we could also enjoy the property from time to time as we travel to the area annually.

But something had to be done, right? So we looked into the prospects of short term rentals. It felt like a much better option and could bring about wealth and social well-being for us and the community as a whole.

As an investor myself, I know exactly what holds you back. Most often it is your fear, your fear of investment, fear of commitment and the biggest of all, your fear of failure. I mean look at me, I have failed far more often than I have succeeded. I've struggled to make ends meet at times and even had to overcome a Bankruptcy to readjust my life in totality. But it is also my moral, ethical, and social duty to overcome my fears and obstacles in life to help leave the world a bit better than I found it especially for my kids.

You must be wondering about how I overcame my own fears. Well, it takes a lot of focus and effort but with time and patience, you will be able to overcome it as well. For easier understanding, I have listed down some of my property investment-related fears and how I overcame them:

Fear of Poor Communication

Every investor is terrified of venturing into a new place, especially when there is a language barrier and so was I. But I made sure to get over my fear by taking the time and learning the, culture, and heritage of the country I was venturing into. I spent an hour a day for almost a year reading about the history of the various countries, the politics and cultural traditions. I looked at Google Maps every day, pretending to explore the cities and attractions as if I was there myself. Trust me, I know it isn't easy but I also know that it is possible.

Fear of Getting Ripped Off

When you're investing in real estate in a village that is located off the beaten path, you are obviously terrified of getting ripped off. It is stereotypical to expect the locals to be ready to rip you off the rich gringo stranger. In particular, when the language, culture and environment is new to you, you feel much more vulnerable. But there is always a solution for a problem, just like there is a way to overcome this fear.

Personally speaking, what I did was to play to my strengths and socialize. I actively started networking to expand my PR and develop contacts with the locals. This allowed me to become familiar with their practices and habits locally, and hardly no time we felt like family. I think by developing strong relationships and networking, I was actually able to prevent the risks of being ripped off.

Fear of Failure

This is the primary fear of any entrepreneur. When you are investing your money into a local business such as AirBNB or short term rentals, there is a lot of livelihood at stake. You are constantly afraid of failure. Questions like "What if the business fails?" can pop up in your mind.

However, an alternative terms for entrepreneur is risk-taker or dream-maker. This means you need to acknowledge that if you want to make profits then you also need to take risks. Once you have accepted this fact, you will actually be able to overcome your fear of failure.

What I did was to work with locals only. No one knows an area better than its residents. So I knew that the path to succeed as an AirBNB or short term rental entrepreneur was to work with the locals. Through networking we were blessed to be introduced to a local Canadian NGO expat who was already doing some of the hospitality business ventures we wanted to do so there was a certain built in synergy already in place. One visit to her education center for kids and a few hours chatting and we were in business up and running. I built a trustworthy relationship with them because I know a business can only succeed if people have some trust and faith in one another.

The reason why I think AirBNB can change the fortunes of a local town or village is because it creates productivity and room for employment. But most importantly, AirBNB promotes local businesses because it allows travelers to experience the local town or village just like a local would.

What's The Plan?

Here is what we are going to do. We have already invested in our bolt-hole property a small, local cabin or 'casa tipica' as they are called in Latin America. We are currently (Springtime 2018) a bit over budget and behind schedule getting renovating the cabin. Our property manager partner on the ground is hiring local craftsmen to completely renovate the place. Once guests get a chance to stay and enjoy some of the amenities we have put in, I think this will be a great way of promoting their local craftsmanship expertise.

We are also collaborating with a local, non-profit women's center director to help us with the ongoing management, maintenance, upkeep and cleaning of the cabin. Again, I believe this is actually an amazing opportunity to provide the local women a chance to upgrade and polish their skills by helping us in the business.

Obviously, there are problems almost everywhere. We have had hiccups with effective communication, but again, our problem solving approach allows us to overcome such ordeals by focusing on what is important: our goals and objectives to improve the village while realizing a decent return on our investment.

We are striving to renovate the place, improve its living conditions, and make it an ideal, local abode for travelers to feel like they are a part of the village. We hope to welcome them to our new home and experience the community as we have experienced it and to enjoy the peace and tranquility living at the edge of the rainforest.

If all goes well, we can expect a 7-15% Return on Investment from our property on an annual basis which is an average yielding for a local AirBNB in this neck of the woods so to speak. But what is more important than the financial benefit is the social prosperity and change brought about from this lucrative investment. Just imagine how many people would get to put their traditional skills into constructive use and earn from their hard work. I believe in a ripple effect so by providing the local craftsmen and women an opportunity to showcase their skills and expertise, we will actually be able to contribute in the growth and expansion of local businesses.

The Future Expectations

Our AirBNB is still under construction as of this writing and we are expecting to finish the project at least by summer. This is also the peak time for traveling so we really hope to complete the project by then to offer travelers a local lodging experience.

Upon the success of this AirBNB business, we hope to recruit more business partners to help optimize and manage their AirBNB listings, we hope to help sell and then renovate a local hotel, acquire another couple of properties and invest in local startup businesses through the women's group. We also plan on educating and training them about the important aspects of business. We plan on educating them about fields such as business building, marketing, accounting, and financing to inspire them to invest more in their own start-ups.

We feel that that what they need right now is training and direction but most importantly, they need proper guidance and mentoring. We hope to give them exactly what they need to encourage them to establish their own, small local profitable businesses that would help them become successful business women.

The aims and objectives of establishing this AirBNB are not just pocketing more and more profits for ourselves. What we really hope to induce is a positive social change by investing in the local villages so that the locals have an opportunity to learn from us and grow, individually.

In this way, they will be able to test their capabilities and strengths. As a matter of fact, when they realize that they are capable of so much, they will feel proud, accomplished, and motivated to move further and beyond. The key to prosperity is the will to do. And by encouraging the locals, we will actually be able to help them put in effect their dreams and aspirations.

Summary

Simply by investing in a local village's short term rentals, we can actually contribute to a whole society's welfare, progress and development. Of course you will have to take risks but it is important to remember that through your thoughtful, managed risk, you will actually be able to profit not just monetarily but also socially and collectively.

Fears are just our internally generated paranoia that holds us back from moving forward. But if we try to get over our fears and think practically, we will be able to bring about a massive positive change in the society through just one tiny step at a time. Work an hour a day towards your AirBNB or short term rental goals and in just six short months, you will see positive, impactful changes in your business and your life.

About the Author

Matt Malouf is a Part Time Investor and Author with a professional degree in BS Engineering from USC. His daytime gig is in Traffic Management and part time business niche is International Real Estate Investing, and Writing.

Matt Malouf has always been fond of writing and helping people. Over a course of some time, he gained the strength and courage to finally pursue another one of his dreams which led him to writing his first book to share his personal experiences with his readers. Matt aims to enlighten the path his readers walk on to learn lessons from his mistakes.

Matt Malouf has introduced value engineering problem-solving techniques to help people achieve their life goals and walk in the wake of success. He is a motivated individual who yearns to expand the horizons of his knowledge.

You can read and review more of Matt's work at:

http://amazon.com/author/mattmalouf

Matt can be reached and consulted through his Clarity account at:

https://clarity.fm/mattmalouf

LEAP AND THE NET WILL APPEAR

"Honey, it's a beautiful day. Why don't you go outside and play with the other children?"

I was raised in Philadelphia at a time that playing outside unattended, in the middle of the street or driveway and being in before the street lights came on, was the norm. Outside was for the less coifed and poised little girls (and smelly little boys) that didn't want to play with dolls and have tea parties in their cute little dresses. But dresses, dolls and tea parties were what I lived for. My Mom was a wife, mother and worked part time at night as a banking supervisor while my Dad worked dayshift. Mom's only spare moment of indulgent pleasure was to quietly read The Daily Newspaper in our Four Seasons porch. I of course would be somewhere in close proximity (like I mean right at her feet), playing with my dolls. One day she decided that I needed to develop a little independence. She sat me on the front steps and latched the screen door. This idea didn't go quite as planned. I kept quietly asking, "can I come in now?" and she sweetly and patiently kept responding, "Not yet honey, you need to get some sun." In my finite childlike mentality, this exchange seemed like it went on for hours. Finally, with the little cherub faces and puppy dog eyes of me and my dolly pressed against the thousands of tiny screen squares, Mom finally gave up the fight and let us back in.

MYTH: INTROVERTS ARE SCAREDY CATS

I'm an introvert with extroverted tendencies by nature. My siblings are much more outgoing and adventurous beings. My parents always presented a united front and decided that I needed to be adventurous like their other offspring – so off to two weeks in the south with relatives, Brownies, Girl Scout outings and summer camp I went. "Surely this will be good for the munchkin" they hoped. After the rounds of hysterics, projectile vomiting and leg grabbing I was sent off to God only knows what horrors that would befall me. They finally concluded that this child enjoyed neither change nor the great outdoors.

Fast forward to everyday life: teenage years, young adulthood, now middle age and not much has changed regarding my contentment with my own company. Some people describe it as fear, but introverts are just more cautious and introspective, comfortable with peace and quiet and feel ill at ease in boisterous environments or large groups. We like to assess and analyze a situation or risk from all sides by sleeping on it if necessary and then make calculated moves. We generally don't just Leap and Expect the Net to Appear.

Even with the feeling of fear being very real and present, after the introvert side processes the level of risk involved, the extrovert side has then been given the clearance to move forward. In business, I'm a fearLESS risk taker and would love to follow my deep desires with reckless abandon, like chasing a balloon who's string has unraveled from its tied post – but, alas, there are others and adult responsibilities to consider first.

FEAR OF NOT BEING ABLE TO SURVIVE...

My Short Term Rental (STR) journey began as a start-stop-start again afterthought. I had been a Landlord with yearly leases on several secondary properties. Then the economy took a downward turn in 2008-09; I got laid off and could barely manage my primary mortgage – let alone maintaining additional ones. I have gone through and am still recovering from property loss, monetary loss, a plummeted credit score and emotional exhaustion. Fortunately, I have a very loving and supportive family. If they had not made contributions to me financially, I would have lost my primary home. Believe it or not, I'm still climbing out of the residual effects of the economic downturn. Trying to find a good paying job at the age of 45 with a mortgage and kid to feed in a location that wasn't paying a decent wage to begin with was a recipe for stress, uncertainty, possible disaster and fear. I had to deplete my entire 401k plan (sans $750) and any other savings type accounts in order to keep my home, have medical/financial benefits from the County for us both and support my child. The best way I can honestly say I managed to deal with it all while trying just to survive day-to-day, was to rely on my spiritual faith, make daily strides to recover the losses and focus on a goal. That goal: Get my daughter off to college. Believe it or not, once that was done, it seemed like I could project all my efforts on getting things back on track. One of the ways I chose to do that was through STR's. As time went on, I heard about a business called Airbnb through some things I had read, signed up, then thought twice about taking advantage of the opportunity because I had a young daughter in my base of operation and backed out. Once off to college, my daughter was the catalyst for my reactivating my Airbnb account and taking things to the next level.

When my daughter would come home for about a month over her school's Christmas Break or when she worked as an RA at the school during the summer and was required to stay in the dorms, she would list her apartment on Airbnb. For her, it was a great side hustle and she only had to occasionally arrange for a co-host when she was away, or apply a little elbow grease to maintain the unit between guests when she was in state. For two years, she kept saying, "Ma, those extra rooms could be making you money!" I finally arrested my fear of the unknown and gave in to reason and started hosting Airbnb guests in my home's extra room, all while still operating my primary Virtual Assistant business (BCC – Small Business Management Services). All gravy and smooth sailing from here, right? Nope!

Once again, my family stepped in to help and donated hard earned cash, furnishings, amenities, blood, sweat and tears and a listening ear in the beginning stages. This is a BUSINESS...not a hobby. Every day I must run my hospitality business with a continuous desire to strive and do better in mind. Each day needs to be greeted with a positive attitude and a focus on providing the highest quality service. It's a daily commitment to the challenge of dealing with people from all walks and cultures. People that were born in a different barn than mine. Some – not all, that I've encountered – don't have common sense, may feel entitled or are just disrespectful of what I am allowing them the benefit of. To some people, my home, is no better than a motel/hotel room that is meant to be overused, abused, disrespected, destroyed and robbed. Most other guest are a Godsend: the guest that is every

Host's dream. But, no matter who books with me, they are paying their hard-earned money with the expectation of staying in a clean and an accurately described/presented convenient space that boasts a gracious, accommodating and knowledgeable Host.

THE FEAR OF 70's HARD ROCK BANDS...

Some STR Hosts have a separate home, apartment, trailer, yurt (or whatever) for rent. Some Hosts rent out rooms in the property that they personally reside in. We are called Live In Hosts (LIH) or On-Site Hosts (OSI). We are in essence, Property Managers (PM) and Owner/Operators. Both situations are a challenge. An offsite Host often needs to install electronic systems to monitor the listing and rely on the help of neighbors, Co-Hosts or relatives, friends or independent property Management Company to oversee the day-to-day maintenance and occupancy. LIH's have the advantage of being within the listing's facility. This setup comes with an entirely diverse set of obstacles and opportunities.

It's one thing to have "strangers" book (rent) my listing and keep my fingers crossed that they will not treat it like a 70's hard rock band would treat a hotel room. But it's a whole other elephant to actually sleep with one or more strangers in my home. There are many boundaries and certain precautions to consider and exceptions to be made; beginning with good house rules, bedroom door locks, in the event guests sleepwalk and putting away EVERYTHING of value or sentiment – that is unless there is a limitless pipeline to the rich relative that will replace lost, broken, stolen or damaged items. It takes a few bookings under the belt to develop a 'Host Gut', that little inner voice that says, that the individual requesting to book my home is "not a good fit". My home is not suitable for children or pets because I work from home (peace and quiet is required and my home is no longer child proofed). Animals don't like my allergies and the possible damage and clean up behind either or both (because parents and owners tend to be lax on vacation), gives me nightmares.

THE JOURNEY OF 1,000 MILES BEGINS WITH ONE STEP...

One of my favorite quotes is, "Start Where You Are, Use What You Have, Do What You Can". That's exactly where I started my journey of converting my daughter's old room into my first Airbnb listing with a twin bed, excellent mattress, like new sheets from a second-hand store, new pillows and other furniture gathered over the years. I toned down the intended earth looking colors (I didn't say earth tone colors) of a teenager's room from green, blue and silver to a very soothing ice gray and a black and white newspaper comic accent wall. My guests love the accent wall that my very creative daughter left behind. I've since updated the room with a full-size bed and different furnishings that I've found online, and at public yard sales or second-hand shops. Hosting seemed such a lucrative venture so I doubled-down. I relinquished my home office in exchange for my kitchen table and began the process of converting another room to a listing all over again. I said goodbye to hot plum walls in favor of a more calming and inviting ice grey. Another full-size bed, all the fixings of a comfortable resting space and it was once again off to the races. [INSERT SLAM ON BREAK SOUND HERE].

Being new to the business, I didn't know quite what to expect. I didn't know I would experience highs, lows, shoulder season, people that were slightly left of center, a towel stealer, an extra people bringer, rule breakers and a lecherous fellow with intentions for unrequited amore, fortunately for me, he was only 1 out of 200 guests. I haven't let these challenges and changes deter my enthusiasm and desire to grow my business to the next level. Patience, persistence, planning and an influx of capital are required to propel me and I'm ready!

FEAR OF ANYTHING SHORT OF 5-STARS…

But I can provide the best customer service personally achievable on a consistent basis. There are many deterrents and obstacles in the Hospitality industry that I like to look at as speed bumps. There are guests that can't be satisfied no matter how much I bend over backwards. They are determined to find something…anything wrong. There are guests who have no respect for my personal property and that just don't give 5-Star ratings/reviews (or any review for that matter). Guests sometimes don't understand or care how critical a 5-Star rating/review is to my continued growth and success. Some guests compare my humble abode or other high-end units to the Ritz-Carlton and will not give a 5-Star based on the hoteliers' standards. It all goes with the territory. A thick skin is required in any business, because after all, it's business…not personal. But wait, hosting is personal. When I have a negative experience with guests, I ask them how I can do better for their return visit or the next guest's, brush off the negative vibes and keep striving because I know that 99% of my guests appreciate all of my hard work and efforts; they show me that in the reviews they write and the care with which they treat my home.

I started this journey crawling as a LIH and now want to graduate to being an off-site owner of property designed for Short Term Rental usage only and now that I have got some time and experience under my belt, I'm looking and working toward that goal. There are so many speed bumps to go over: capital, financing, location, furnishing, remote management, marketing and booking but when I feel that moment of fear like bile coming up in my throat, I swallow hard and control my breathing and look at the goal posts. I can't score if I don't kick.

RELINQUISHING THE FEAR OF SUCCESS…

Airbnb and HomeAway (and their affiliates) and Inclusive were the first three platforms I selected initially based on referrals. I've since altered that selection. I looked at a few others but did not like their sites, terms, conditions or methodologies. Along with these (and soon to be other platforms), I also use various social media sites including Instagram, Twitter, Facebook, Tumblr, Hashtags, networking events and opportunities and special promotions to market and promote my listings. I also reach out to previous guests with a "hello" and offer repeat stay and referral discounts. These are the first few steps in my long-term plan and journey to dissolve my bad debt and to acquire additional property to increase my net worth and portfolio. Remember the Tortoise and the Hair or the Younger and Senior Axe Men stories? In both instances, slow and steady (with wisdom) won the race. Working hard, continuous education, mentors, helping others and applying tried and true methods will help me work through and use any fear I may, particularly the fear of being successful. The concept of success is an unknown and therefore, presents an opportunity for fear to creep up and rear its ugly head.

FEAR IS A JEALOUS & GREEDY LOVER...

I wake up to them every morning and go to sleep with them every night. They are hateful lovers; greedy, self-loathing, self-centered, manipulative and all consuming. But I also wake up and go to bed with love, grace, peace, hope, positivity and a new determination that I will take steps each day toward my objectives and goals. My Dad always said, "If you go on your feelings, you won't get out of bed in the morning."

Years after I stopped watching Sesame Street, the show still resonates with me. One thing that I realized much later in life was that the creators were not only teaching children the basic in numbers, letters and being neighborly to people that don't look like ourselves but also attempted to assuage children's fear of monsters by making them cute, soft, furry, friendly and loveable. That way children would learn to embrace their fear of monsters that went bump in the night. As an adult, I can use the same metaphor for life's fears … embrace the fact that some things may cause us to be afraid, get comfortable with facing the fear head on and maybe, just maybe they are not as legitimate as our imagination built them up to be. After all, fear is based in not knowing the unknown.

DO IT… AFRAID!

Each time I'm about to host another guest, it's as if I'm in labor all over again. When will they arrive? How much longer to the finish line? Who signed me up for this? Did I meet and exceed their expectations? Will they leave me a good 5-Star review? But before I can dwell on it for too long, it's time to get ready for the next guest. The first date butterflies begin all over again. But, checking my bank balance after each guest's payout helps me quickly get over any fears or anxiety about why I started this journey in the first place. Is there an unpleasant side to all of this? Do some Hosts report horror stories about damage, theft, destruction, blatant disrespect of Host and their property? Yes! BUT… those are the exceptions and not the rule. Every advance in history has a negative undercurrent associated with it. This may never be my experience or your experience and therefore we should never let the fear of what could or could not happen guide our decisions in life. Nor should fear keep us from diving into or continuing in the Short Term Rental world.

Believe it or not: fear could have kept me from writing this chapter!

P.S. I still don't like change or the great outdoors.

You don't need to know where you're going if you know God is already there.

About the Author
CRYSTAL L REED

Crystal L Reed has been in the Marketing & Sales arena for over 25 years. She has worked for H.J. Heinz Co., StarKist Foods, Inc., Heinz Pet Products, Mountain View Community Church of Temecula and KinderCare Learning Centers. She was born and raised in Philadelphia, PA, and in her last year of high school, moved to Los Angeles, CA. After college, she embarked upon her career with Heinz and relocated to Cincinnati, OH/Newport, KY until 2000. Crystal then returned to Southern California where she currently resides with her family and operates business endeavors which include BCC - Small Business Management Services (Business Concierge, Virtual Admin & Social Media Support, Event & Networking Coordinator), A Suite Collaboration (Hospitality Services), Crystal's Jewel Persuasion (specializing in Medical Alert/Regular Jewelry) and Jamboree of Unstoppable Networking Women (Networking, Training, Education and Celebration of Women Entrepreneurs) and Public Speaker/Motivator/Encourager. Her deepest passion is mentoring and coming along side women of all ages to encourage and promote them during their personal journeys and entrepreneurial endeavors. She loves comedy and romantic movies, talking to her dog, dancing like no one is watching, car dancing, singing loud and off key in bumper to bumper traffic and throwing her head back in knee-slapping laughter. She is currently in a new phase of her life's journey...empty-Nester and she is now opening her heart, life and home to all of Life's and Love's possibilities.

============

CONTACT:
951.777.0255
P.O. Box 141
Murrieta, California 92564-0141
bccsbms@gmail.com
http://www.BeCrystalClear.net
http://www.Facebook.com/BCC – **Small Business Management Services**

The Accidental Hostess

Like most of the activities that have defined my life, I fell into Airbnb hosting by accident.

My husband Howard and I were looking for property in the Sierra foothills of Northern California. We were hoping for a special place, not only offering the acreage we desired and a bigger kitchen, but at least one 'extra' as well. Several potential sites had either outbuildings, fenced pastures or 'granny units'. We settled on a house that had a beautiful one bedroom unit attached to the garage, along with everything else we loved.

The guesthouse had one bathroom attached to the bedroom, a full sized kitchen, living/dining area and a laundry room, packing quite a punch into 600 square feet.

I wasn't sure what I wanted to do with it. I think I was just in love with the potential. It would be a great place to accommodate friends. We could rent it out for extra money. Or we could explore the idea of a short term rental.

We had a long escrow which gave me plenty of time to think. I began to love the idea of the short term rental model as it would allow us to share our home when we wanted to and not share it when we didn't. The house could still be available to friends at times of our choosing and the income potential was most likely greater than having a long term renter. It we didn't like it, we could simply shut off future reservations.

It seemed so easy, but was it? I pondered all the potential negatives. Would it be too hard to keep clean? Would guests trash my pristine little peace of heaven? But I think the biggest concern I had was that I would invest money into the preparation and no one would want to come out to where we were located. We are in a lovely area but we are off the beaten track. I really was unsure of what to expect, even though I had seen many listings for my area. I was going to have to have faith. One thing to keep in mind was that if no one came out that far, I'd still have a cozy little retreat of my own.

I'm not impulsive. I tend to mull ideas around in my head for quite some time to the point of procrastination. It was no surprise to me that months went by without any movement in the direction of hosting.

In the end, hosting my sweet little unit won out. I was having far more positive thoughts than negative, and I realized that I gone through the same mental process in my head in other areas of life.

When I first started my pet care service many years before, I had never pictured myself an as an entrepreneur. I had always worked for other people. But I had an idea germinated from helping friends care for their pets. I would fantasize about the great service I would provide and I would run the numbers of the potential income. I achieved those first goals to the point of needing to hire help. I did the mental calculations on what my new earning potential would be with the higher volume I could accommodate. When I was training to qualify for the Boston Marathon, I spent many long runs planning on just how much I could slow down due to fatigue in the last miles, and still finish with a fast enough time.

All of these scenarios had negatives, but the positives always won out. I'm goal oriented, but I know it's not enough for me just to have them. I have to believe. I have to envision success and see it playing out my head. These positive scenarios I rehearse in my head help me do that. When my mind is set, I'm a force with whom to be reckoned.

This project was not just about the income for me, although it was an intriguing carrot being dangled in front of my eyes. It was about the experience. I wanted to create a moment in time in which my guests felt well cared for in a peaceful environment, a place of calm and relaxation. One of the reasons I loved my pet sitting service was the positive feedback from my clients. Income has always been secondary to customer satisfaction. Without that, it all seems pointless. I don't just provide pet care. I sell peace of mind.

My goal is for my clients to travel worry free knowing their pets and home are in good hands. I thought about those concepts and that feeling of comfort. I considered what I would want in a home away from home and what I would need to do to get that positive feedback. I set out to create just that.

I had a good canvas with which to paint the pretty picture in my mind's eye. The guesthouse was in excellent condition, just nine years old, and only lived in for a short time. I did need to purchase appliances. The refrigerator came along quickly when we moved into the main house, and while I thought and rethought about this whole rental idea, the gas range was something that took me months to finally purchase. The laundry room had space for a stacked washer and dryer. I was finding it a challenge to locate one with the right dimensions. Only about 20% of the models I saw online would fit, and price was a definite factor for me.

As luck would have it, someone advertised a used washer dryer combo in a local online forum. It was in excellent condition and could be mine for just $350. It was a defining moment for me. Now there was no longer a gaping 'hole' in the space, begging for an occupant. The laundry room was now really a laundry room. And it seemed all at once that the pieces were in place.

The excitement was building. I began to purchase more towels, artwork for the walls and small appliances, such as a toaster, for the kitchen.

There was just one thing left to do: get set up on Airbnb and list my little home.

As a worked through all the details of setting up my listing, I realized I still had some trepidation. Was anyone going to drive out to my home to stay? I was 20 minutes from the freeway in most directions. If I could lure guests out my way, would they complain about the roads? The last quarter mile to my home is a mix of gravel and pavement, mostly gravel. My driveway is steep and all gravel. There are lumps! It is truly a bit of adventure they first time one comes to my home. Scratch that...driving up my driveway is an adventure every time! There was only one way to find out if this was going to be an overwhelming obstacle. I would simply be up front in the description of my property. I had researched our town and found other listings not far away. I believed I would get bookings. I just had to hope the total experience would negate potential negative reviews on the roads.

It was with both excitement and a little bit of terror that I completed the process of setting up my listing. Within the first 24 hours, I had my first booking for ten days out.

I scrubbed the place from top to bottom in anticipation. I found little shampoo and conditioner bottles at the market and set them out with fluffy towels. I added some new pillows to my bedding. I attached a lockbox with key to the door. I stocked the refrigerator with breakfast foods. I had bread, butter, bagels, cream cheese, juice, milk, coffee, creamer and my favorite offering, eggs from my own chickens. (My 'girls' have presented me with a range of colors, from green to blue to dark brown eggs.) I put chocolates on the pillows. I made my first draft of my house manual with some key instructions that might be needed. I made sure to communicate with my first guests about where to park and to let them know I was reachable should they have any questions. Then I took a deep breath and hoped for the best.

My first two bookings were each one night, back to back. I quickly realized that I had set my set myself up for a challenge with only a two hour window in between check out, noon, and check in, 2 PM. But it was manageable and I decided to leave it as is for the time being, because I was still not convinced that I had a popular spot for bookings. I had also priced my unit very conservatively. I knew I could change it later as this whole thing was kind of an experiment anyway.

When my first two reviews came in with five stars, I was elated and somewhat surprised. I had felt that I had a good handle on what constituted an amazing experience but seeing my fantasy become reality was better than I expected. Not to assume it was going to continue to be easy, I scouted stores for more decor that would finish my look. It was still a work in progress as I set about to make a cozy home with a French country style. I replaced an ordinary light fixture in the bedroom with a delicate yet rustic chandelier to add to the look.

The bookings continued to come in. My first December was almost filled to capacity, as I had Christmas and New Year's week reserved by holiday travelers.

I added a chalkboard sign so I could welcome my guests by name with multi colored chalk. If I knew there was some sort of celebration or event, I would mention that in my message. These are small touches that cost very little and yet the impact was big.

What I had not anticipated was the number of friendly people I would meet.

It was often just a wave, but sometimes a nice longer chat.

The topic that broke the ice for many was my small herd of Nigerian Dwarf goats. We often let them free range on the property. They often come over to the guesthouse to say hello. They are friendly, like dogs, and almost everyone has mentioned how fun they are.

The animals I'm able to share with my guests do round out the experience I was hoping to provide. We have 10 acres, about half of which are easy to navigate.

The chicken coop is accessible to my guests and I encourage them to stroll the grounds.

We are currently renovating the area in back of the unit. We have fenced off the area so our adolescent dog does not disturb anyone. This provides a separate backyard for our guests. We are adding pavers and plan to have enough plants to create an English garden feel.

In just six months, I have hosted about 40 groups. I have raised my price slightly, and changed my check out and check in times. This has not resulted in any noticeable change in booking numbers. The 34 who have left reviews have all given me 5 stars. My success in hosting has fueled a desire to do more. I want to keep improving my current listing and I'm starting to have a notion of expansion. I don't see it happening right now, but I have another fantasy of buying a little house somewhere just for short term rental. I have so many doubts about that! Just like I had doubts about running a pet sitting service, running the Boston Marathon, and renting out our guest house. So time will tell!

My tips...

Have faith and picture success in your mind. Then you can believe!

Envision the amenities that you would want if you needed a place to stay and provide that and more. Small touches can mean a lot without costing very much.

About the Author

Born in 1960, Kim Ottone Tank grew up in the town of Salinas, California, where she met and married her husband Howard in 1982. Always surrounded by animals, she worked as a registered veterinary technician. Six years later, they moved to the Walnut Creek area, and in 1990 Kim took a leap of faith and started a pet care service, still in operation today. It was a busy time as she and Howard started their family, totaling four children by the time they were done. Owning her own business was something Kim had never imagined doing. Finding success, she began to imagine what else might be possible. In 2007, she took up  running, after never previously having been athletic. Less than two years later she ran fast enough to qualify for the Boston Marathon and has since run the famous race 5 times. In 2016, she and Howard decided to fulfill their dream of moving to the Sierra foothills. It was there she found her dream house which included a beautiful one bedroom 'granny unit'. The wheels in her head began to turn with exciting possibilities. By late 2017, she was off on a new adventure that of being a short term rental host. Kim takes great pride in providing an excellent experience for her guests. She has found it more enjoyable than expected and is glad she took yet another leap! She currently divides her time between her work in the San Francisco Bay Area and her home in Pollock Pines, California where she lives with Howard, her oldest son Joel, a dog, three cats, 6 goats and 32 chickens.

My Harmony Hideaway

"Roll the Dice!" "Take the Risk!" Over the course of my 47 years on this planet, I have taken risks. Big Risks. I lost more times than I have won but have won more in those few times than I lost in the others.

I have been blessed with a family who supports my decisions but every venture I have done I went at it on my own… until now. Now my wife Linda and myself are 50/50 partners and share the responsibilities in our new Short Term Rental and I love every second of it. Two years prior to the purchase of our property I took a bad beat on a business that was successful for over a decade, won local awards, put food on the table, and allowed me to live a humble but fantastic life with my family. I walked away with debt that was not generated by myself but by a partner and I had to struggle to get it off my balance sheet.

I turned to Real Estate as an agent to make ends meet as well as driving a school bus and working in a restaurant. I did everything I needed to do to get back on my feet and I am not above doing any job out there. I needed to make money so I did. Then came an opportunity I couldn't pass up, Short Term Rentals. Just toying with the idea of buying property to rent out as a STR I started looking for the perfect property and was shocked when I found it. We wanted to buy in a vacation community in the Pocono Mountains of Pennsylvania where we would vacation every year since my youngest son Eric was born and when we did find the perfect property, sadly, we couldn't afford it. Since not being able to do something doesn't make me stop, it was time to figure out how it could be done.

We looked for the perfect home that we could afford and we when we did find it, it wasn't in the community that we wanted and loved. The house was affordable and we could make it work so we settled and made the offer. The 3 bedroom home was going to be ours when the homeowner accepted verbally. We signed the contracts right away but homeowners did not.

The contracts just sat there and expired because the homeowners were away on vacation. When they came back new contracts were generated however, we had changed our mind by that time. We didn't want to to settle. We wanted in the community we loved and we would find one. We would not settle. We would find a way to get what we wanted, where we wanted. Fear tricked us into making that offer and settling and I allowed fear and doubt to lead me. Since my roadblock was the fact that I couldn't afford market value homes, I looked for months until I found one at market value but was on the market for a very long time. I made the below market offer and got the deal. We were elated to get a house for that price, nothing could be better, nobody was better than us! Then the fear set in.

In the past, every time I attempted a new business idea, we always had money saved. It was our safety net. This time around we had all our money into the investment. No net, no safety. Success or complete failure were the only two ways that it could go and with my oldest son Brian about to start college, there was zero room for error.

Figuring out a way to buy the house for an investment should have been the hardest part since I spent most of my time on that subject, but it wasn't, not even close. The fear was. What are we risking? What if we are wrong? What if we are right but the laws change? What if we are right but more people list their homes for nightly stays? What if? What if? What if? The term "What if?" is, in my opinion, the most dangerous phrase in the English language. It causes doubt, fear, and worse of all, a delay in making your decisions. The emotional rollercoaster that you ride is unlike any other and causes further delay, doubt, and fear. It was such a vicious cycle that we decided to pass on the deal, keep our money secure, and wait until a better time.

Now that the decision was made and we decided would save up our money and try again in the future, we could relax so Linda and I opened a bottle of wine. We spoke about the time when we made another difficult decision of me opening my first business. In retrospect, I remembered advice I received from a respected friend. When I asked what would happen if I failed and lost all my money, his reply was simple. "You get another job and pay it back." So simple, so basic, so true.

What if? What if I failed turned into what if I succeeded. What were we risking turned into what will we gain. What if we were wrong morphed into what if we were right. What if other people listed their homes for nightly rental turned into pity for them if they tried. That night, after hearing echoes of advice I had heard over a decade before, it was time to roll the dice!

The next morning papers were signed and we were in contract and on our way to a new way of looking at life. That decision that night changed the entire trajectory of our life goals and our plans for retirement but first was the hard work of starting our new business because this was now a true business.

The happiness and excitement took hold as we planned our STR. We made lists, watched how to videos, and planned and dreamed. It was all cupcakes and rainbows and we looked forward to it. The fear still sat in the background, but we controlled it.

The day of the closing when we paid all that money for a property that may net us a 15% return on investment or bankrupt us, fear returned. The amount of work was beyond our comprehension. The mountain of repairs, the scale of the remodeling, the scope of the work and time needed hit home. Yes, we "knew" what to expect but "knowing" is a lot different than what we experienced. Living it. As we sat in our new home, our old friend fear walked in the front door, poured itself a drink, and started laughing as it sat down in between us. We bet everything and it was up to us to make it work.

Money we had budgeted quickly ran out so fear drove us to work harder at our other jobs in order to get the capital to make the improvements. Anxiety dropped in to say hello when our timeline ran over and we were missing our ski season and the income we projected it would generate so we worked even harder and faster. The miles on my car increased with each 2 hour drive to the house to get stuff done and check on our contractor Ken who is also a family member. Ken was a god send and saved the day and we were ready half way through ski season.

Valentine's Day arrived at the same time we were ready to start renting. That was our true test. Our cleaning crew Diane and Michele (Linda's cousin and Ken's wife and daughter) went in for a solid cleaning to get it ready. Linda and I went to spend Valentine's Day in our new investment with a Hot Tub, Fireplace, and all around retro feel. We walked in as guest. With us walking through the door was Fear, Anxiety, and Doubt. This is the moment when our life changed.

Up to this point, every time we were at our investment property was for work. Ken was there improving the physical house, Linda was improving the decor, I was doing everything in between. The house was always dirty, dusty, and no fun to be in. Getting a STR up and running is a dirty job and the home reflected this. Then Diane stepped in and gave us our STR named "Harmony Hideaway".

As Linda and I stepped through the door with Fear, Anxiety, and all of their friends something happened, all the emotions changed. The home was clean. Not just any kind of clean but the kind you can feel in your bones. The home was amazing. Diane did an amazing job. Fear and Anxiety were kicked out by Happiness and Joy and we prefer those emotions over the first. Our home was perfect and we were ready to rent. We made the right decision. As we were sitting on the couch in front of the fire, Linda looked at me with a smile and said "Now we need to buy one on a beach!"

About the Author

Kevin Borgersen was born and raised in New York City where he still resides today. With his wife Linda and two teenage sons Brian and Eric, the family enjoys long road trips, amusement parks, and most of all food festivals. As a serial entrepreneur he has purchased existing business, ran startups, and has also closed failing business. His best success after leaving a management position in Corporate America was as an independent owner of a children's entertainment facility that won multiple local awards in categories such as "Best Party" and "Best customer service"

Eager to try new things, he has also run business from exercise gyms to online sales platforms, has worked in both the corporate and private sectors, and has done everything from piloting an airplane, to SCUBA diving wrecks in the oceans of the world.

Kevin and his wife Linda purchased their first Short Term Rental in December 2017 in the Pocono Mountains in Pennsylvania and are currently planning on purchasing their second in a beach vacation community. The plan is continue to purchase Short Term Rental properties wherever they like to vacation and when they retire they can flow from one property to the next and enjoy the golden years traveling.

Visit Kevin's rental at: https://t.vrbo.io/s85PigKvMM

Kevin Borgersen, Realtor

Herman & Co.

7319 Amboy Rd.

Staten Island, NY 10309

718-757-1384

No Time for Fear; Too Busy Making Guests Happy

By Katharine Hansen, PhD

Starting a new business is scary. The risk factors are enough to frighten any would-be entrepreneur. But what would it be like if NOT starting the business was an even scarier proposition?

That's the position I found myself in back in September 2016 when my husband completely blindsided me by telling me he was divorcing me and moving out of state. How would I support myself? I had a small income from online teaching, but it certainly wasn't enough to maintain a 40-acre farm.

Thus, I was terrified. In a 32-year marriage, I had become rather dependent on my husband. Would I have the will, strength, wisdom, and guts to find a way to make it on my own?

One idea was tickling at my brain. I was fortunate that we had two homes on our property. We had purchased the adjacent property shortly after moving from Florida to Kettle Falls, WA. We didn't really need a second home, but buying the contiguous property would help maintain our privacy and perhaps be a good investment.

I had worked slowly on re-modeling the second home, which is a double-wide modular, with the idea of turning it into a short-term rental (STR) someday. At the time of my husband's bombshell pronouncement, the house was probably a year away from being STR-ready. My fear settled in as I contemplated how to support myself in the meantime.

Then, my soon-to-be ex made a suggestion that I'd like to think I would have eventually come up with myself: Why not turn the primary residence into the short-term rental? Eureka! I certainly didn't need to be rattling around by myself in a four-bedroom home. Having been built in 2009, the house was in much better condition than the modular home was. It could sleep more people. It would need very little work and time to get it in shape.

I moved into the modular home and got to work in the STR-to-be converting an office and a fitness room into bedrooms. My ex even built me a set of bunk beds for one of them!

As I prepped the STR, I began to conquer my fear of managing the physical space. I was handling it! But a whole new set of fears creeped into my consciousness. I live in the rural boonies, outside a tiny town with a population of 1,600. Who has ever heard of Kettle Falls, WA? How would people find me? Who would want to come to this obscure area? Would I actually get any bookings?

I listed the place on Airbnb, with the intention of starting to take bookings about two months hence. "Opening day" was to be Nov. 13. I got my first booking starting Nov. 14. That was encouraging, but it didn't quell my fears that bookings would be few and far between.

The rest of 2016 was slow, but by about February, the bookings engine was humming along nicely, and summer was almost completely booked.

Where were these guests coming from – since I was so sure no one would ever find or want to stay in Kettle Falls? I had anticipated that my guests would be mostly families taking in the recreational aspects of being near a National Forest and a National Recreation Area along the Columbia River. In the summer, that was the case, but the rest of the year, I had all kinds of guests – couples seeking a getaway, family reunions, people in town for a wedding or graduation, writers' retreats, a nuns' retreat, business people, folks looking to buy real estate in the area, hunters, boaters, and anglers. I was surprised that most my guests are from Washington, many of them from as close as Spokane, just 2 hours away.

My biggest amazement, however, came from how much people seemed to love my place. No guest we'd ever had in the house when we were living there ever said anything about how the place looked. But my STR guests rave about the décor. Contrary to current trends, I adore bright colors. You can tell me till you're blue in the face that white walls are more marketable, but I will never change my brightly colored walls.

I've had 5-star reviews since the very first booking. 100 percent. I became a Superhost the first quarter I was eligible and have remained one. The volume of bookings I got went a long way toward helping me past my fears and making me feel successful, but it was the reviews and accolades that truly jazzed me. Ask me today my definition of success, and I'll tell you in two words: Delighted Guests.

I am not analytical and not a numbers person. Many STR hosts would probably be aghast at my amateurish bookkeeping and the fact that I have reinvested quite a lot into the business. But I measure my success in happy guests. As long as I can pay my bills, I consider myself a financial success. I know many STR-ers would balk at my lack of emphasis on profit, but it works for me. I believe that if I continue to put my guests first, I will experience both financial and emotional abundance.

Further, I am constantly looking for ways to make them even happier. When guests arrive, they are greeted with a seasonal wreath on my front door. Once inside, they encounter a welcome card and bottle of wine, as well as some sort of flowers or a potted plant. Early on, I bought fresh flowers for guests before I realized what a costly practice that would be. In the spring and summer, my area is riot of wildflowers, so now I just cut some of them. I leave a small supply of breakfast items to get them started. I added a firepit and a "FirePit Fun Kit" (s'mores supplies and powder that turns the fire colors), as well as puzzles and games.

I believe the circumstance of moving out of my family home to turn it into an STR has been part of its success. While I removed virtually every personal item, what was left behind made for a much more "like home" feel than some STRs. It's not sterile. It's engaging to look at. I left behind books, DVDs, CDs, art, and knickknacks. Some hosts would eschew the "clutter" and fear theft, but since the contents of the house are working for me, I'm sticking with them and have decided nothing in the house is worth getting upset over if it gets broken or stolen.

The "former family home" aspect also makes it especially well equipped. In a review, a guest said, "If you can't find it in this house, you don't really need it." The kitchen is especially well supplied and offers unusual small appliances, such as an ice-cream maker.

Interestingly, Airbnb's new Plus program has motivated me to go further to delight guests. Now, I have no illusions that Plus will come to Kettle Falls in my lifetime (I'm 64). But I'm still motivated to make my place Plus-worthy. Plus hosts, for example, can't have any beds that are directly on the floor, so I got a bed frame for my one bed that was like that. I've upgraded my bedding. I have a wish list of other Plus requirements I want to meet.

I still have fears about cleaning and maintenance, especially because I do my own cleaning. I was mortified when I once forgot to clean the shower, and guests pointed out the dreaded human hair in the drain. Anytime a guest makes a complaint I consider complaint-worthy (aforementioned hair in the drain, surprise ant invasion, hair dryer not working – even though it actually was), I give a token refund of $25. The gesture is worth it to me keep guests happy. However, sometimes I get carried away. Recently, I fully refunded a guest who complained of no hot water. I assumed the water heater had gone on the fritz. The hot water was fine when I went to clean the next day. The guest's wife must've had a heck of a bath or shower that used up the supply. But the incident did push me get my act in gear to upgrade from a 55-gallon water heater to an 80-gallon so that the larger groups arriving this summer don't have to wait for water to reheat between showers.

I have moved so far beyond my fears and attained such a high from delighting guests that I am itching to expand. I was approached by a couple of camping versions of STR platform, so I developed 6 campsites that are available for booking this summer (one booking so far). Next summer, I want to turn the shop on my property into a bunkhouse. I'm intrigued by possibly doing farm stays and inspired by a guy in a Facebook group who uses his property for a sport called "trail-running."

But the biggest twinkle in my eye right now is the property about a half mile away that I am now under contract for. After all, even if you are fully booked year-round, you have only so many nights in a year, so the way to expand is with more properties. I stumbled across this new property accidentally and felt it was affordable. The land is amazing, with a creek running through it. The house and cottage on the property will take some work, but remodeling is truly the fun part for me. The place offers lots of intriguing rental combinations and is close enough to my existing STR to handle overflow groups from that listing. I can't wait till I close on the property and can start listing it.

In Summary ...

My story is about how I turned fear into success – which to me means delighting guests.

My 3 fears and how I overcame them:

•   Fear of not being able to support myself: I targeted a path I was already interested in – becoming an STR host – and found a way to make it work optimally.

•   Fear of failing as an STR host for lack of bookings: I focused on customer service and creating a wonderful experience for my guests. Certainly word of mouth, great reviews, and repeat guests have been a major part of my success.

•   Fear of not measuring up in terms of cleaning and maintenance: I continue to do the best I can and get cleaning tips from the various STR social-media groups. For example, a Facebook group recently had a thread about hosts offering barbecue grills. One commenter remarked on what a pain they are to clean. Ulp. Clean? Would you believe it never occurred to me to check on whether the grill had been used and clean it? I also give small, token refunds for legitimate complaints.

Key Takeaway for STR Hosts

Concentrating on making guests happy can distract you from any fears you have about your STR business, and when the 5-star reviews come rolling in, you will know the satisfaction of giving others a wonderful and memorable experience. A little adrenaline can be a great motivator, but don't let your fears keep you from the success you deserve. Keep looking for the next way to thrill your guests.

About the Author

Katharine (Kathy) Hansen, Ph.D., is a online educator, author, and writer, as well as a 5-star SuperHost on Airbnb. Kathy, who earned her PhD from Union Institute & University authored You Are More Accomplished Than You Think, Tell Me About Yourself, Dynamic Cover Letters for New Graduates, A Foot in the Door, Top Notch Executive Interviews, Top Notch Executive Resumes; and with Randall S. Hansen, Ph.D., Dynamic Cover Letters, Write Your Way to a Higher GPA, and The Complete Idiot's Guide to Study Skills. Kathy teaches online classes for several universities in organizational leadership, organizational behavior, management, social media, business/managerial/organizational communication and more. She also serves as a dissertation-committee member for several PhD students in organizational leadership.

In 2010, after living her entire life on the East Coast, Kathy moved to Kettle Falls, WA, where she runs a 40-acre woodland farm with dogs, goats, chickens, and a pony. In 2016, Kathy turned the main house on this property into an Airbnb venue and has been far more successful than she ever imagined she would be.

Kathy is extremely active in the Toastmasters organization, a worldwide nonprofit educational program that enables people to sharpen their communication and leadership skills. Kathy has held many offices and roles in the organization and recently led a district comprising 800 members as District Director. She holds the highest distinction offered by Toastmasters, the Distinguished Toastmaster award.

Kathy's favorite activities include creative pursuits, such as repurposing furniture and creating unique wall hangings. She also loves to bicycle through beautiful Eastern Washington, identifying wildflowers and snapping nature photographs. She also thrives on constantly improving her Airbnb rental business and finding new ways to delight guests.

http://www.katharinehansenphd.com

MY JOURNEY TO HOSPITALITY

I first used Airbnb in the summer of 2015. As a solo traveler, I wanted to interact with the locals, and I figured an Airbnb's private room would bring this opportunity. I was not disappointed and greatly enjoyed my interaction with the hosts and other locals. After two more Airbnb stays, I decided to venture into Airbnb hosting myself. I launched my first listing in January of 2017.

Prior to my third Airbnb stay during New Year's 2017, I had just purchased a new 3-bedroom home, and this trip was a reward to myself after a 9-month journey of house hunting. My plan was to stay in one room, have a roommate, and host guests in the other room. I thought this would provide me the best combination of a steady income and flexibility.

Brian, my third Airbnb host was a Super Host with 250+ reviews. Super Host is a badge granted by Airbnb for hosts who provide extraordinary experiences for guests. As I told him about my house plan, he wasn't hesitant to share his hosting experience including the good, the bad, and the ugly. The worst thing that happened to him was a guest stealing his wine and smoking marijuana inside the house while he was out of town. I reassured myself that if that was the worst thing which happened, then I could be a host.

Besides our conversations, Brian invited me to come along to his neighbor's New Year Eve party with him and his boyfriend. He even gave me food to bring to the party. His hospitality was exceptional, and the room was nicely decorated and comfortable with amenities like a TV, iPad and balcony. However, after 5 days of staying there, I gave him a 4-star review because of a minor noise issue. I regret it. If I have known what I now know about Airbnb's star-based review system, I would give him five stars. Airbnb's star-based review system is different from hotels. Airbnb penalizes hosts who regularly earn four stars or less as it is considered these a service failure. This trip was not a service failure in my eyes. Thanks to Brian, I was confident enough to start down the road of becoming a host and eventually a Super Host.

My first listing was not very sophisticated. The room was furnished but not well decorated. My listing had a brief description with five pictures. There wasn't any amenity, house manual, or guide book. I had some blurry vision of how I'd like the room to look - something soothing, relaxing and harmonious. After searching for an impactful artwork above the headboard, I found a 48x72 canvas of the beautifully balanced Taj Mahal. Everything else was designed around it. I chose the earthy tone of beige, brown, and yellowish to match with the painting and named the room Zen.

My first booking happened only one day after I listed the room on Airbnb. I started with a lower price than nearby places. It was one of Brian's tips for starting out, and it proved to be well-founded advice. As I did more research on hosting, this same pricing suggestion came up many times. It is an effective way to attract guests for brand new hosts. My first booking was for six days. I remembered telling myself "Wow! it works".

Over time, as I added more things and built up my reputation through reviews, I increased the price accordingly. I got many compliments from guests about how beautiful the room was. Anytime that I am asked for interior design advice, my recommendation is to start with a focal point of a painting or a special piece of furniture. A design is only fun and unique when it is personal.

In addition, I also suggest using a contrast of dark and light colors. For example, if the comforter is grey or brown, the flat sheet or the pillow cases should be white or beige. When they are put next to each other, they complement one another. Using a focal point and contrast makes the space visually appealing. Since the Zen room, I have designed five more rooms, but somehow it is still my favorite. This may be because it was my first complete interior design project, or it may be because I loved every minute of its creation.

My plan of having a combination of long-term and vacation renters didn't work well. My roommate, Iris, was a 17-year-old international student who had just come to the U.S. for 3 months. She had a boyfriend who came to my house every day. They cooked, talked, and ate together. He normally stayed until midnight. I told her that I could only allow her guest to come to the house three times a week and stay until 10 pm. In my Airbnb's house rules, the quiet time is 10 pm till 6 am, so I wanted everyone to follow the same rules.

Iris and my guests shared a bathroom. One weekend, she put too much paper in the toilet and it became clogged. She called her boyfriend to come over, but he couldn't fix it. They left the clogged toilet and went out. She did not tell me. I had a guest, Jane self-check-in right after that. Jane couldn't use the toilet, so she had to go, and use the toilet elsewhere.

The next morning, I offered Jane fresh coffee and pastries as an apology for the inconvenience. When my service is not up to the standards promised, I go a little above and beyond to hopefully make up for it. Based on my experience of hosting 200+ groups of guests, the investment of a little extra normally goes a long way. When I am sincere, take actions to remedy issues, and make up for them, most guests forgive, move on, and leave a 5-star review. They might write about the issue in the review, but it would end with positive remarks. Those kinds of reviews are the best as they show me as a helpful and reasonable host.

Circling back to my roommate, I ended the tenancy and converted her room into another Airbnb guest room. This combination of long-term and vacation renters could work with the right roommate, but Iris wasn't the right fit. I find most Airbnb guests are respectful and polite. And if there is a difficult or disrespectful one, this person will be gone in a few days. This is a flexibility that I would not have with a roommate.

As I got deeper into hosting, I became more passionate about it. It was the joy of being an entrepreneur who provided a service to people. I read lots of blogs, articles and books. I listened to podcasts, browsed places worldwide on

Airbnb website and watched YouTube videos. I wanted to know all the dos and don'ts to attract more bookings and receive more five-star reviews.

Anytime I learned something new, I applied it right away. The thought process I followed was: Ok, that sounds like a good idea. I haven't done that yet. Let me add that to my listing. I tirelessly thought of my business, and how I could improve it day in day out. At times, I added too much text, and my listing got cluttered. Then, I would reevaluate and delete some of the information.

To make this chapter easy to read, I classify the hosting process into four phases: first impression, booking, before the stay, and during stay. For each of these phases, I have learned many lessons.

Phase 1: First impression

The first phase is when a potential guest enters Seattle as location, private room as the property type and dates on Airbnb website. My listing then appears among hundreds of other listings. This is before they read the details of my listing, so I call it the first impression phase. To make my listing stand out so that potential guests click on it and read further, I focus on creating an attractive profile picture and a title highlighting the unique selling proposition. If a picture is worth a thousand words, a profile picture is worth a million words. People are more gravitated toward a picture than lengthy text. The profile picture must represent the listing at its best.

The second thing a guest will see is the title. My first title was "Seattle private room near Link light rail". It was redundant and ambiguous. First, guests already picked Seattle and private room in the filter. I did not need to remind them. Second, near is a subjective term, and it is not descriptive enough. Then, I changed it to "Zen, spacious & 5-minute walk from Link light rail". The new title was better. It provided a unique selling proposition for the room (i.e. calming and roomy). However, some guests mentioned that it took them 9 minutes to walk to the station. As I realized some people walk slower than others, I updated the tittle to be "Zen, spacious & 3 blocks to Link light rail". No one would argue about the distance phrased in terms of blocks.

Phase 2: Booking

This phase is from the time a guest starts reading my listing to the time the guest sends me an inquiry or a booking request. An inquiry is a pre-booking message. To get the conversion from browsing to booking, I describe in detail every component of the listing including a summary, a description of the place, guest access, interaction with guests, other things to note, and the neighborhood. I called my house Happyhouse for easy reference. It is also how I want guests to feel when staying there.

For pictures, I stage each room and wait for a day with natural light to take photographs. I provide plenty of bright, clear and beautiful photographs so that guests can imagine themselves in my Happyhouse. One hidden feature that I did not know until recently is photo captions. Most people use it to describe the space. However, it is more effective to describe an experience that could happen in that space. For example, instead of writing "stainless steel appliances and granite counter top kitchen", writing "Tired of eating out? Why not make a home cooked dinner in this fully stocked modern kitchen with stainless steel appliances and granite counter top?" is much more effective. The idea is to create an inviting image that a guest can visualize partaking in.

A host profile is also important. At the beginning, I had a very short one. When I learned that guests have more trust in hosts who are more descriptive about themselves, I updated my profile. Airbnb does have some suggestions about host profile such as originations, job, travel places, etc., but I found them boring. I wanted my profile to be exciting, inspiring and real – something that is truly me and can be a take-away for guests. So, I wrote about my favorite activities of dancing, reading, traveling and hosting; what I have learned through them; and how they have benefited my life.

Phase 3: Before-stay

Before-stay is the time from booking confirmation to arrival. This is when more communication happens between hosts and guests. Normally, guests are most concerned about check in. They want to make sure that they can get in. This is why check-in is one of the ratings that Airbnb has for guests to measure hosts. My process includes a house manual sent to their emails two weeks prior and a message on the Airbnb application asking about their estimated arrival time one to two days prior to their arrival. A detailed house manual is a fantastic way to remove guests' concerns, not only about check in, but also parking, layout, WIFI, and other details. It also helps guests to familiarize themselves with a new place prior to their actual arrival.

Phase 4: During stay

This phase starts with a check-in and ends at check-out. To make check-in smooth, I installed a smart lock for self-check-in. I equipped the space with things that are convenient for guests. There is a luggage rack, a body mirror, an organizer, an extra pillow and blanket, travel magazines, a surge protector with outlets and USB ports, and night lights with sensors in the guest room. I also set up night lights in the bathroom and hallway, a brochure rack, and a snack area in the kitchen dedicated for guests. I label things in the shared area for clarity. I check with guests during their stay and thank them at check out. I thought that was enough for physical comfort and convenience.

My business was going well. I kept receiving 5-star reviews with compliments from guests. For each month of the summer, I made twice my monthly mortgage payment. Feeling satisfied, I stopped trying to be on top of reading every Airbnb news article and blog post. I told myself that I did an excellent job, and there wasn't much more room for improvement until one day I was further inspired.

I hosted Shelly who was traveling to interview to be a flight attendant with Alaska Airlines. She was a little tense, so I invited her to sit in the living room to chat. She opened up and told me her life story. She joined the military to try to escape the grief from her father's passing. They had been each other's best friends. It was good at the beginning. She was surrounded by people and felt less lonely. Gradually, as she healed from the grief, she realized military life wasn't for her. She did not foresee herself being in the service for the rest of her life. She wanted to leave in order to travel and see the world. So, she applied to be a flight attendant. She hadn't been in an interview for more than seven years, and she was nervous. She was doubtful about her ability, and she was scared of changes. We talked for two hours. We felt connected. When she got up and went to her room to rest, she thanked me for listening and making her feel more relaxed.

The next morning, before leaving for work, I sent her a text to wish her the best. Around noon I got a message saying that she passed the first round and other candidates gave her compliments for a good performance. Apparently, the first round was a group interview. Alaska Airlines wanted to see if candidates could interact well with one another. I wished her good luck with the second round. By the time I left work, I received the message that she passed and got the job. I was ecstatic. It was like I was the one who passed the interview for my dream job.

She left the next day to go back to the base. On her bed, I found a box of yellow "Happy Is…" note cards inside. I was touched. At that moment, I realized, happiness to me is when I can "Leave people better than I found them" — **Marvin J. Ashton.**

As I acknowledged there was another level of service, something more than just a clean, beautiful and convenient accommodation, I met Danny Meyer. To be correct, I did not meet him in person. I met him on YouTube. His video about hospitality was interesting, so I picked up his book "Setting the Table" about the power of hospitality in restaurants, business, and life. It was revolutionary.

To give you the context, I grew up in a developing country of Vietnam where service was not as strongly emphasized as products. I have a degree in Engineering which is more of a left-brained logical and analytical field. I knew nothing about service and hospitality. When I read Danny's definition about hospitality that "Hospitality is present when something happens for you. It is absent when something happens to you", I felt it in my heart. I kept coming back to that quote while reading the book with a desire to clearly understand its meaning. It resonated with me. I was impressed with the amount of effort his staff put in. They remembered customers' names, birthdays, special occasions, favorite tables, favorite dishes, and the last times the customers ate there. They went above and beyond the normal definition of a restaurant (i.e. selling food and drinks). Instead, they sell emotional comfort. This distinguishes them from everyone else and made them many people's favorite.

Since discovering Danny Meyer, I have become a more responsive and informative host. I know I have a good "product" of accommodation. By focusing on the interactions between my guests and myself though, I am able to make memorable experiences that go well-beyond five-star reviews. I have found that it takes a tremendous amount of mental strength on my part to give others emotional comfort. This is also what it takes to bring my business to the next level though. My journey to hospitality is the journey to a better self.

About the Author

Thao was born and raised in Ho Chi Minh city, Vietnam. She developed the love for books and arts at an early age. She read lots of comics, novels as well as painted for fun throughout her tween and teenager's life. She moved to the U.S. in 2005 for her graduate degree in Engineering. Caught up with school, work and life, she forgot all about her hobbies for a decade. In 2015, she moved to a new place in a new city. Her apartment was close to the  public library. She started reading again and felt much joy. She also started journaling to relax, reflect and recharge.

Thao began hosting Airbnb in 2017 and found herself deeply enthusiastic about it. It suits her personality as a domestic, personal, curious, compassionate and polished kind of person. As an introvert, she enjoys small groups and big talks i.e. meaningful conversations and Airbnb is a great platform to do so. It has brought the world to her doorstep without her traveling around it. From 1 room, she expanded to two and now she also cohosts for other people's properties.

She continuously reads articles, listens to podcasts and scribes about hosting. As her seniority with Airbnb has grown, she wants to share her experience, knowledge and wisdom to encourage people to open their front doors for others. She believes that the world will be a better place if everyone is a host as it shortens the distances, removes the barriers and brings people all together.

Visit Thao at: https://abnb.me/xazQVNuwMM

The Reluctant Host

I never wanted this job. But now, I'm addicted to hosting. The first thing I do when I wake up is log into my Airbnb and VRBO accounts, check my rankings and update my status. I daydream about staging new photos. I study up on thread counts and mattress firmness and the best stain removers for towels. I fixate on how many steak knives I should have. I live for the trilling of the phone app, notifying me that I have a new inquiry.

That's now. Let me tell you about then.

I come from the frozen North, and I've always yearned for sun. I visited Central America about twenty years ago, and on an evening stroll through a picturesque town I saw pictures of homes with thatched roofs plastering the window of a real estate office. I was hooked. I set my sights on owning a beachfront home in the Caribbean when I retired.

I hoped, I worked, and I saved. I took more than a few vacations and tried on more than a few Central American countries. Gradually, I narrowed my search to Belize, a tropical, beachy, friendly country that felt like home from my first visit. Then I zeroed in on Ambergris Caye, or as the singer Madonna called it, "La Isla Bonita." I began looking at properties, and in 2008, I found a one-bedroom beach bungalow condo in a soon-to-be-built resort that seemed perfect.

My first mistake was investing in a pre-construction project. I thought I was being careful, and in the beginning, I probably was. I talked to other investors and acquainted myself with the basics of Belizean property law. I hired a Belizean attorney, and made sure the developers had clean title to the land. I negotiated a contract with stage payments, and made arrangements to verify construction steps in person before releasing funds. I thought I had done all the right things, and all I had to do was watch my building go up.

But I made a second mistake. I got way too friendly with the developer and his wife, and I started to trust them. We had dinner together when I came to the island. Our kids played together. We chatted on the internet when I was home in the United States. I let down my guard.

They called me one day with excitement in their voices. They had a potential investor who was insisting he wanted the condo I had already purchased, but they had an offer for me they thought was a win-win: they would put me in another condo unit, a two-bedroom, a few yards north and closer to the beach, for just a bit more than I'd contracted to pay for the one-bedroom. They would get another sale, and I would get an amazing deal. They had me at "closer to the beach." I signed a new contract, and paid them more money.

But on my next visit, when touring the construction site with the developer, they pointed to a shell of a building on the south of the site, far from the beach, indicating it was mine. I knew it was not the condo I had agreed to buy, and incredulously asked what was going on. There was a flurry of apologies and excuses, whispered negotiations, then another offer: because they had made a "mistake," and already re-sold the condo I was supposed to have, they would move me to a three-bedroom place, even closer to the beach and just a bit farther north, at almost no additional charge. I forgave them and signed another contract.

What I didn't know was that the building they had moved me to was on a different parcel of land than the first building, and this parcel of land was heavily mortgaged. So when the developer and his wife were arrested for real estate fraud a few months later, I wasn't nearly as protected as I thought I had been.

The next several years were a rollercoaster. The developer and his wife went to prison, and construction stopped. Eventually, some of the other buyers who had signed purchase contracts but had nothing to show for it rallied and took control. A handful of new investors stepped up to try to complete the development. The builder soldiered on with new business partners, but it wasn't easy going. Rumors of failure flew around the internet. The new investors struggled to convince buyers like me that it was safe to make payments, but many felt they'd be throwing good money after bad. Construction proceeded at a snail's pace.

But snails do move. After a few years, the investors completed a few more buildings, managed to put in a restaurant and swimming pool, and the resort opened its doors. I visited, and I loved it. But, I had no place of my own yet. For another couple of years, I wondered each day if I had lost my life savings or not.

Some of the others with purchase contracts are still on that rollercoaster. I ended up being one of the lucky ones, in large part because I finally took a leap of faith: I made another stage payment. The new investors came through, and my condo was completed in 2014. While I didn't yet have title, I was permitted occupancy (title came over a year later – another story).

So now I had a place to rent out. Condo owners in this development, titled or not, were permitted to join a rental pool if they desired. The resort management promised owners 65% of the gross income, with the remaining 35% going toward advertising, management and upkeep. With on-site management, the owners could sit back and let their properties earn them money, even from thousands of miles away. After all we had been through getting our places built, many were ready to reap those rewards. Still, initially I resisted – after all I had been through, I felt a bit territorial, and I didn't like the idea of strangers sleeping in my bed. But, I had racked up lots of unexpected expenses in the six years it took for my condo to be built, and it really was a sweet deal, income with no sweat. So after a while I relented, and put my condo in the rental pool.

At first, I made just enough to cover my homeowners' association fees. That was really all I wanted, and I would have happily continued that way for another ten years until I could move to Belize permanently. But, I didn't anticipate the politics of a homeowner's association. I was an absentee landlord, and the board controlled both the resort and the rental pool. Within a year, my HOA fees more than doubled, and my rental pool earnings dwindled.

Others in the resort had their condos listed on short-term rental sites, in addition to being in the rental pool, and they were making money. I didn't want to do that. As reluctant as I had been to join the rental pool, I was extremely reluctant to become my own advertiser, manager and host – I already had a full-time job in the U.S, and a busy family. But, I finally relented and listed on AirBnB and VRBO.

At first, I sucked at hosting. I put up a few pictures that I had taken with my cell phone, penned a very short description of my place, and waited. Of course, nothing happened. And after several weeks of nothing happening, I forgot to pay attention. So, when an inquiry finally happened, it got lost in my email inbox. For weeks, I just plain didn't notice it. And when I finally did notice it, I had no idea of the impact of my neglect. It wasn't long before my place was at the bottom of the searches.

I'm amazed I ever got another inquiry, but eventually, I did. Someone actually wanted to book my place. I wanted to click the "accept" button right then and there, but I couldn't, not without running the inquiry past resort management. The problem was that I was still in the rental pool, and had no idea if the resort already had a booking for the requested dates. The resort office was not open 24/7. So, out of necessity, I waited.

If I'd known then what I know now, of course I would have responded to the inquiry immediately, if only to tell them I'd get back to them. I naively did nothing until I could confirm that the rental pool hadn't already booked my place. By the time I replied, the potential guest had moved on. I'm embarrassed to say I did this numerous times, and still didn't understand why I was falling in the rankings and failing to get bookings.

Meanwhile, my rental pool earnings were falling even further and money was getting tight. I started wondering what was afoot. I searched the resort website and online travel agencies for a three-bedroom place that slept six, and it offered me three one-bedroom condos instead of my three-bedroom. I cried foul, and was labeled a complainer. Didn't I know that if I had searched for a one-bedroom place for six people, my place would have come up, because it is one rentable unit? No, I didn't know that, and I'd bet neither do guests. If you had six people, would you expect to search for a one-bedroom rental? My frustration with the pool deepened.

The last straw came when I found out that a guest had stayed in my place for ten days, and I got absolutely no income from the stay, while others in the rental pool had payouts that month. The explanation was that they counted earnings based on the day the guest left. My renter had left September 1st, and September earnings were too low for a payout to the pool. But, the other owners who had people in their places for nine days in August got nice payouts. Too bad, so sad, I was told. Needless to say, that explanation didn't fly. It was time to get out of the pool.

That was when I put on my big girl pants and started to work at this business. The first thing I did was take a big step back. I took some time, and really thought about how I could become successful. After all, if I wouldn't open a restaurant without learning to cook, I shouldn't be renting my condo out without learning how it's done. So, I googled. I studied. I watched YouTube videos. I found groups of others who rented, and who supported each other with advice and encouragement.

At first, some of the advice for improving rankings irked me. I was supposed to update my calendar every day, even if nothing had changed? I should rearrange my picture order, just to show I was paying attention to my site? I didn't like it. I couldn't figure out why the system rewarded people with higher rankings for fiddling with their listing in a non-meaningful way.

But, like it or not, that was the system, and I had to learn how to use it. So, I thought about what made my rental unique. I thought about the type of traveler I wanted to attract. I revamped my listing descriptions, with an eye toward key search terms. I took new photos, with higher resolution. I shared my sites on social media, and I asked friends and family to like and forward.

I religiously visited my listings, and added and changed and deleted and putzed. I started to get bookings.

And, that's when the fun began. I found that I really liked interacting with the travelers and being a tour guide. I know my island well, and it's fun to answer a simple question like "What's the best restaurant in the area?" with a detailed description of the amazing seafood wontons and chaya dip I had the last time I ate at Finn & Martini's place on Back Street (shout out to Finn!).

I also love that I can make someone's stay better by sharing my ten years of experience in the tropics. For example, if you want to prevent sand flea bites, just slather on a little baby oil and those fleas won't be able to get a grip on you to bite. If you forget to oil up and they do bite, just rub a lime on it and the itch goes away.

Soon, I was sharing my knowledge with potential guests, and sometimes even with those who had inquired but booked elsewhere, just for the fun of it. I started enjoying the interactions, and I started going to the short term rental sites just for fun, and tweaking my listing just because I was there and I had an idea.

That's when I started getting five-star reviews. And that's when I finally realized that people appreciate a host that cares, and hosts that care fiddle endlessly with their listings – which meant that those arbitrary requirements to move up in the rankings by paying attention to your listing were not so arbitrary.

So, what have I learned as a successful short-term rental host? I've learned that you're either in or you're out – you can't just throw up a listing and wait for the money to find you. But I've also learned that if you care about the guests and get excited to share your experiences with them, then it won't be work, it will be fun.

Retirement from my day job is coming soon for me, but I'm realizing that I don't want to retire from the short-term rental business. I'm heading back down to Belize soon, to look for another property. No more reluctant hosting for me, I'm in.

About the Author

I am an attorney from Wisconsin. My day job finds me regulating health care facilities and advising government entities. At home, I have a man and two adult sons whom I love and am very proud of. Between us all, we have a tribe of pets, including two dogs, three cats, and three parrots. The parrots swear like sailors. I'd blame my sons for being the bad examples, but that's just not true. It's me.

My short-term rental is a three-bedroom, three-bathroom ocean front penthouse on the island of Ambergris Caye, in Belize. The condo is two stories, on the third and fourth floors of the building. We have five private balconies, all with amazing views of the second-largest barrier reef in the world. We're surrounded by lush, tropical jungle. Secluded and peaceful are the most common comments from guests.

You'll find me on the more common short-term rental sites. Mention that you found me here, and I'll take 10% off your rental in September, October or November!

https://www.vrbo.com/762596

https://www.airbnb.com/rooms/7885018

https://www.rentals.tripadvisor.com/6791508

Choosing to Be the Best

Looking back on what has led me to where I am today, I can't help but think of the roads I've taken, - or not taken, - and how experiences formed me into who I am and how I think today. When I think about what it is that guides me in operating our short-term rental, I think back on advice I've received in the past. This advice has had a common denominator: Do things right! In one instance, I recall this advice coming from my high school metal shop teacher, Ronald Turner. Mr. Turner was not only our teacher but also a skilled craftsman. He had an interest in restoring antique cars and located a 1935 Chrysler in a junkyard. It wasn't exactly accessible, so he and a crew dismantled the car where it sat and carried it out in pieces! The parts were carefully restored and assembled by his students in the school shop. Mr. Turner taught us the finer points of bodywork on that car, utilizing molten lead in the old-school tradition, - although that would violate OSHA regulations today. One day, he must have become frustrated with one of the other boys in my class and I overheard Mr. Turner telling him, "If you're going to build something, build it the best way possible! If you're going to be something, be the best there is! Even if you're gonna' be a bum, then lay there, - do nothing – but be the best damn bum there is!" Even then, I understood that Mr. Turner was using humor in trying to impart his wisdom, but that piece of advice managed to stick with me. I have since found that there is no excuse for being second-rate when one can instead put in the extra effort to be the best. Often, all it takes is to practice a skill or a task and to even let yourself make some mistakes. Learning from those mistakes is what makes us better. This philosophy came into play when we set up and began to operate our Short-Term Rental on a daily basis.

As with much of the things we learn, not all of this advice comes from the classroom. For example, my father was a carpenter, - one who built things to last and who was never satisfied until any task was done to his satisfaction. He led more by example instead of through deep conversations, so I can't recall any "Rules To Live By" that I would have received from him that stood out over the years. But still, a few things do come back to me now and then when I am working. I remember as a youngster helping him on weekends sometimes when he had side jobs that he would take on in addition to his weekday construction job. Sometimes we would be repairing a home where we required ladders and staging to work above the ground. His rule for safety was to always have a sturdy staging on which to work. He'd say, "Even when they used to hang a man from the gallows, they'd build a strong staging so he wouldn't get hurt on the way up." Now, this was a long time ago when he told me this, but even then public executions had long since vanished from the landscape. But if you think about it and apply that same work ethic (with a few adjustments) to everyday jobs, this too can be a useful tool. Everything we do needs a good foundation or it will fail. Even when we think about beginning a Short-Term Rental venture, a solid business plan is important. Building a team that includes a tax professional, tradespeople who can make repairs when needed, and cleaners (if you aren't handling that yourself) is essential before you collect the first dollar of revenue. So, even though my dad passed away fifteen years ago, I still find myself adhering to some of the rules he laid down so many years ago. I didn't know it at the time, but he was teaching me many of the skill sets that I still use to this day. And it all boils down to Doing Things Right. Shortcuts just weren't his style. In the same way, while shortcuts can be an effective way to lighten the work load of running a Short-Term Rental, we need to make sure that these shortcuts don't cheapen the end result, - the final product. While we can find the quickest to do the turnover of a room or property, it does no good to skip steps in the cleaning process, for example, just to save time.

Something else that has stuck with me and which I think about on an almost daily basis actually came from a very unexpected place. Ever since I was a young teenager, I've been crazy about cars and auto racing. That interest eventually settled into following the sport of drag racing. I have never owned or driven a race car, but I really liked travelling to the nearest sanctioned drag strips which were each about two hours away. The most exciting of the professional classes at the drag strip are the nitromethane-burning Top Fuel Dragsters and Funny Cars. When I was a kid, these cars could be campaigned by families instead of the mega-buck teams that exist now. For some it was a hobby but for others it was a business. One such team consisted of a driver named Charlie, who might have been about twenty-five years old, and his dad who appeared to be old enough to be the kid's grandfather. After each round of competition, service needed to be performed in the pits on the cars and the engines. In that era, money and spare parts were extremely limited and these people needed to learn to make everything last in spite of the extreme stress the equipment was under. When Charlie's Fuel Dragster returned to the pits following one run, it became apparent that the engine had suffered some damage in the form of a burned piston. As I walked through the pits, I could see Charlie's dad under the engine surveying the damage. Suddenly I heard his dad yell out, "Charlie! Get me a piston!". Charlie went into their enclosed transport trailer and I could hear the sound of random objects being moved or tossed around. Charlie called back, "Which one do you want, Dad?", to which his impatient father snarled, "The only one we got, Charlie!!!"

I thought that was a funny exchange between those two, but the old man must have already known that they were down to their very last replacement piston for the racecar and they had better make it last. I know that doesn't sound like sage advice, and for many it wouldn't be if they managed to miss the real message there. My take away from that is that every one of us, whether we are racing a fire-breathing racecar, running a business, or operating a Short-Term Rental (which is its own type of business), needs to have the supplies on hand that we need on a daily basis. Redundancy is the key. It really helps to have a ready supply on hand of consumable goods as well as multiples of the things you need to operate. Since we happen to live in the same property in which our Short-Term Rental is located, if anything (like a coffeemaker, vacuum cleaner, or dishes) breaks we can easily swap out something from our own home. My point is to be ready for any reasonable thing to go wrong and have a contingency plan for it. When I was young, I was proud to be a member of the Boy Scouts. As I'm writing this, I can't help but be reminded of the Boy Scout motto: Be Prepared! I think that counts as one more piece of advice that has helped me not only in life but also in running a Short-Term Rental.

When my wife and I were married, we eloped to the beautiful state of Tennessee and spent a week in the area of The Great Smoky Mountains and the cities of Pigeon Forge and Gatlinburg. This a truly beautiful part of the United States, and I encourage everyone to think about spending some time there. This trip was before the advent of platforms such as Airbnb, but my wife was able to find a website for a real estate agency that managed various homes as Short-Term Rentals. Part of the time we spent in the area was in a beautiful chalet in on the side of a mountain. There were other such homes nearby, some I'm sure also used as Short-Term Rentals. The individuals and families who built these properties must have had the best of both worlds. They could have income from the rentals, but still have a beautiful home to vacation in or to spend their golden years in during retirement. This was a few years before we purchased the home where we now live, but even then I could see how sweet the setup was that existed there. Now that I think of it, maybe the seed was planted in my head during that trip. The idea that operating a Short-Term Rental is a viable option for someone whether they live in the home, as we do, or host remotely, as we saw during our Tennessee trip.

Although I like to believe I can learn something from every new experience, I think the advice I have gathered over my life has served me well in accomplishing what we have here today. I don't think I'm done learning by any means. But one thing is for sure, - I am glad we've added a Short-Term Rental business.

About the Author

Thomas Blouin is a Home Improvement Contractor living in Portsmouth, Rhode Island.

Tom and his wife operate a Short-Term Rental apartment in their home, just steps from the salt water of upper Narragansett Bay. Before starting his Contracting business and, later, their Short-Term Rental venture, Tom had a career as a trucker transporting commodities of almost every kind. As Rental hosts, they really enjoy meeting people from locations near and far. In addition to hosting guests from around the U.S., as well as from other countries, Tom and his wife, Cindi, like to pick places to vacation that are new experiences for them. Seeing our beautiful country and experiencing what it has to offer are their favorite ways to relax. Maybe someday they will expand to foreign destinations! Tom and Cindi have three adult children.

Visit Tom at: http://tcbproperties.com

AFTERWORD

I would like to extend a heartfelt thank you to each of these co-authors for making a dream of mine come true with this book project. It has been a few years in the "thought processing" stage and wasn't until recently that I got the kick and jumpstart to take all the ideas and just move them forward. To turn ideas into action and reality. Each of these co-authors took a leap of faith, to trust a guy they met on Facebook with an idea and a proposal to possibly achieve a bucket list item. For that faith in humanity, that faith in me, I am forever grateful. I set hard and short deadlines for this project and everything in here might not have been perfect but the stories and lessons shared are perfectly helpful to those who take it in and I hope this book project has helped you in some way.

I envision this entire project to be eight volumes in total, if you would like to contribute to one or more of these volumes please reach out to me on my new Clarity page https://clarity.fm/mattmalouf and let's chat more. We live in the sharing economy today and part of that means sharing anything and everything we care to share, especially our life lessons and experiences. Personally, I found this project to be very inspiring and soul fulfilling, it was a lot of fun and I met some absolutely incredible people here. I believe we can all benefit and help each other on our journey to short term rental success by sharing our stories from the edge….more to come, very soon! What do you have to share? More than you think, contact me today.

www.ingramcontent.com/pod-product-compliance
Lightning Source LLC
Chambersburg PA
CBHW031538210526
45464CB00003B/1066